Make Yourself Great Again!

PART II - THE ACTUAL WORLD I: HOW THINGS <u>REALLY</u> WORK

An Introduction to Mindset Stacking™ Solutions.

by **Dr. Robert C. Worstell**

Table of Contents

BONUS

Special Cheat Sheet Study Guide for This Part 2 is Ready For You To Download.

(for a limited time only)

Instant Access

Click or type into your browser:

http://livesensical.com/mygajoin/

INTRODUCTION

(Continued from Part I)

This story has everything to do with you. It's about how you stacked your mindset into the shape it's currently in.

Any failure, any melt-down, any blow-up, any mental crash you've had is all on you.

Sorry, just the way it is.

The environment around a person is the result of their actions, which are started by their thoughts.

People think in recurring patterns, which confirm the mental habits you already set up.

When you stack your mindset on static facts, you are building in a future crash. The ancient Polynesians said, "Any truth is as valuable as it is workable." And so the later Greeks and Romans developed a term called "philosophy" which can be understood now to mean "love of things that work."

Facts are tied to time. They erode, they become less workable.

Meanwhile, people change and improve their minds constantly, this is called "learning."

People who don't "learn from their mistakes" are doomed to continue doing the same things over and over, but expecting different results. As Einstein said, this is the definition of insanity.

And so, their mindsets crash and leave them vulnerable to using other programs (called emotions) to play out. You see people hysterically sobbing, weeping, wailing, and this is what's happening. Their emotional programs have taken control of their actions.

(I've covered how to reprogram your emotions in my earlier books, see Appendix, and we'll touch on this again in a few chapters.)

This part of our journey has to do with the discovery of villains. Those creatures who are wittingly or unwittingly making your life harder and more complex than it needs to be.

We need to start out examining this new world, the actual one we live in, not the "real" world which we've been trained to believe.

And it's our "beliefs" that hold the keys to the locks we want to open. Because our beliefs tend to create what we consider as facts. Most of us build our mindsets on facts. So if we want to make a more resilient mindset, we need to examine what we believe and why we believe them.

Unfortunately, we'll also see that our beliefs are stacked in a manner that keeps them from being examined easily. This is part of our culture, and again the way we've been trained to act.

Before we can uncover the true villains, we have to find out how to find them, how to uncover their trail.

There are many, many false trails out there as well. You'll find yourself more than once doubting your own sanity. And, of course, doubting that I'm telling you the truth.

This part, as the whole book says this one piece of advice:

Test everything you hear, read, or view – *especially* what I tell you here.

Only then will you regain your certainty. And that is the sole route to a resilient, bomb-proof mindset.

HOW TO GET YOURSELF SCAMMED - AND SURVIVE

Living on a farm, you don't expect some scammer three states away to serve you with a legal form.

I was on the phone with a friend when an off-duty deputy rolled up in an unmarked car. So my friend held on while I went out of the farmhouse to see who that was.

The deputy asked me who I was and then handed me a manila envelope.

I'd been served.

Back inside, my friend on the phone was helpful. He told me about a kit I could get to explain how to deal with legalese.

It took awhile for the shock to wear off, through.

- - - -

Let me back up. All I'd been trying to do was to work out how to earn extra income online. Passive stuff was best, like how to sell the books I'd written and self-published.

In those days, the raging thing was eBay. This was before Amazon was anything. You used to be able to sell digital books on eBay, which changed just as I got into it.

I'd been punching along on the Internet, signing up for various things in order to get data about how to crack into volume eBay sales.

Unwittingly, I'd given my credit card data online for a $1.95 download + $3.95 shipping for a couple of CD's. (Of course I found a month later that they were trying to charge me for a $39.95 monthly fee to have access to a worthless site. Yes, I got that canceled.)

What happened next was someone called me (yes, I gave them my phone, too - but wait, it gets even better...) and that guy started asking me:

- What did I really want to accomplish with that eBay data - would I be interested in a course that could tell me all about how to get what I wanted out of it?

- Well, yes.

- OK, then. A guy I work for would like to call you. Let's set your appointment...

The next day I spent over two hours discussing with this guy all about how eBay worked and this great company he worked for where "every one was an expert eBay trader" and could help me set up a site with everything I needed to get going.

It only cost me several thousand dollars on a credit card, but he guaranteed me I could make it all back in 30 days. And repeated that last several times.

Guar-an-teed.

Some days later, I got access to the site and found out that it didn't exactly work that way. It was going to take me three months just to get through enough of their training to get *started* on building a website. Meanwhile, their site builder was pretty dated. I could do (and had done) better on Wordpress or even Blogger.

When I started to complain, I was kicked upstairs to someone who got me to continue on the basis that the company had "merged" (his words) with a new company who would be taking over my training.

So I got a new trainer. And told him I already had plenty of experience in website building (I'd supervised the roll-out of a 30,000 page website for the Syndicate in the late '90's.) So

I asked if I could build my own site on a Wordpress back-end. He said, sure, go right ahead. And then I got that monthly billing canceled for the hosting.

Then I went back into their training and found they had really stupid lessons once I got to the point of picking out stuff to sell. None of this was really going to get me rolling to the point of making sales on eBay any better than I had before I signed up for that training. Essentially, I realized that I knew more than they were able to teach me.

But I was already out those thousands and had been paying that card off for over four months already while they were trying to keep me on board.

So I hit the refund route, again.

The support guy tried to keep me on board, but the bottom line was that they said Utah (where they were based) had a 3-day right of return law, and they weren't required to do anything after that.

I was stuck to either being a good boy and finishing their training, or doing something else.

That was the beginning of the end for them.

I fired up my research and blogged what I found. All sorts of things came up. I found a prescription for refunds which essentially said: Complain Like Hell - Everywhere You Can.

Being a nice guy, all versed in self-help, I took it a step further. I laid out and wrote up all the exact steps to take, and all the places people needed to file their complaints, starting with the FTC, FBI, FCC, and then working down to the State Offices in both your state and Utah. Oh - and make sure you send a copy to the Governor and A/G of that state as well (Utah had a very nice online complaint box for the Governor there.)

I also set this up so anyone could get this list of places easily, with hyper-links and everything.

Then, I told them to pay if forward and help five other people get their refunds - Golden Rule stuff.

I also posted this Refund Recipe on not just my blog, but every single complaint forum I could find.

What was ironic is this scammer company was depending on it's stellar rankings on the front page of Google which all said how great a company it was. Meanwhile, they were teaching their students how to research on the Internet.

Unwittingly, that spelled their doom.

Within a month or so, the listing for that scammer training company had been pushed off the front page of Google and had been replaced with a dozen complaint forums as well as their bad BBB listing.

What this list of actions also did was to flood the Utah Department of Consumer Protection with all these reports. And I do mean flood. My posting on those complaint forums had the long list of places to complain to. Those places all seemed to forward everything to that Department for resolution.

I also wrote a few books based on my research and blog posts, and gave them away for free. Put them up in places where they could be found and downloaded for free, all licensed as "share and share alike."

Within two years, I'd gotten my refund and helped 10 other people get theirs.

That's what resulted in my being sued by that scammer company, and having to agree to take down my blog and forum postings as part of my settlement. But not before other people were already spreading the same list of steps over and over.

A few years later, the company registration was pulled by their own request. That company didn't exist any longer. Ironically, their name was Thrive Learning Institute.

And if you want the full blow-by-blow of how it went down, with all the recovered blog posts, I've set these all up for free download (you don't even have to give an email – see Appendix.)

But what does this have to do with beliefs and success?

Mainly that this was the second time I'd been badly scammed, and I thought I knew my way around.

The key part to this was how I dug myself out and who I found to help me.

There's this psychology professor Robert Cialdini, who had gotten a bit tired of coming back from stores with more things than were on his shopping list. A friend came in one day as he tells it, and asked him why didn't he just take them back. Cialdini replied, "Because I'd wind up coming home with even more."

So he started studying what they were doing. 12 years of research later, he came out with a book that's been in print ever since and through several editions. It's called "Influence". The purpose was to help people recognize these 6 techniques sales people used and proof them up so they didn't have to buy stuff they didn't need or want.

The funny point is that people started using his book to work out how to influence others. There was so much demand for it, he had to write a sequel.

I'd first read about Cialdini's 6 Points of Influence when I was studying up on "Internet Marketing". Of course I figured it was another scammy technique until I actually got a copy of Cialdini's book.

The techniques were good, they were effective. But while anyone could actually learn how to become "scam free", scammers now had a textbook they could use to improve their "conversions."

Well-intended research was being twisted to the dark side.

Now this didn't answer all the questions I had about getting scammed.

Another widely-touted idea was that there were two basic motivations for human behavior: pain and reward. This really stemmed from some very old studies Freud had done on crazy people. And anyone who's covered psychology even slightly knows there's a lot more data out there than that simplistic view.

So I dug in - and along came Abraham Maslow and his studies of motivation. Maslow started at the other end. He studied people who were operating at their peak, and the successes they had, plus what made them achieve better than anyone around them. His breakthrough paper in the 1940's essentially laid out a scale of motivational behavior which went from mere subsistence (just staying alive at all) at the bottom to self-transcendance (existing only for the benefit of others) at the top.

Now we were getting somewhere.

From the side, I'd been sent some material about Lester Levenson. His story was one of being home to die and was told to not even get out of bed. That was their solution for severe cardiac problems in his day. But as he had an active mind, he pulled himself up into a chair and started thinking. Three months later, he had essentially cured his heart problem. And meanwhile, he had achieved a high state of existence that it took him another 18 years to figure out what he had done.

What he had uncovered was a simple way to release things that are bothering you. They are usually along the lines of wanting or wanting to escape from: control, security, or approval. Just find these and let them go. And then they quit bothering you. Yes, it's that simple. (See links in the appendix for more data.) Just recently, I ran across a book by Catherine Ponder who recommends the same actions. In order to get more prosperity in your life, she says, you have to let go of the things that are holding you back. Her idea is that you create a "vacuum" by getting rid of things you've accumulated, both physical and spiritually.

Now we had the solvent for the glue that was sticking all these scammer's efforts to you. Cialdini had the intellectual side figured out. And Maslow could explain why you did things. Levenson (and Ponder) showed you how to simply release them.

This means anyone and everyone can get scam free. (Yes there's a free book for you with that title also linked in the appendix. You're welcome.)

Why do you need this stuff?

If you start looking through your life to find out who is trying to control you, force you to approve, or threaten your security, then you start finding who is actively working against your success.

Make a list of these and you may be surprised. Or not. They are pretty blatant at it.

But if you practice releasing regularly, and then work up your skill at this to be able to release every moment during the day, you'll acquire a skill that will take you a long way.

In fact, this is one of your key skills in sorting out your beliefs so that you can succeed all you want, at whatever you want, to be whatever you want to be and have whatever you want to have.

WHAT IS WRECKING OUR LIVES AND GIVING US FAILURES?

For every conflict internally and out in the world at large, there is always a villain.

We don't know at this point who ours is, how to identify them, how to send them packing and be free of them.

All we know is that someone or something is constantly working against us. Or this scene would have dissolved long ago.

Beliefs are weird things. They come and go through a person's life. Beliefs can be changed, as they really seem to be nothing more than mental habits.

This doesn't explain how they can crash a person's whole life.

People have literally worried themselves to death from the beliefs they held.

And others have had incredible lifetimes, filled with excitement and treasure.

What is the difference here?

What affects some people one way and yet changes others completely different?

There is villainy afoot.

We know it exists in our own mental world, right "between our ears."

That means we know who this is.

Our job is then to find out how, and why.

Unless we change something, we'll do this for the rest of our life.

Or we'll simply keep doing the same thing over, and over, and over. Stumble, fall, get back up, then stumble and fall again...

FLIPPING THE UNBALANCED COIN OF SUCCESS

There is a coin of success. Flip it and you can tell anyone's future.

The trick is that one side is 10 1/5 times larger than the other.

In our society, there are a few numbers that repeat. One of these is the tiny number of people who will make a success out of their lives and the huge number which simply goes along with everyone else.

Earl Nightingale said this in 1956:

> "Let's take 100 people who start even at the age of 25, do you have any idea what will happen to those men and women by the time they're 65? These 100 people believe they're going to be successful. If you would ask any of these if they wanted to be successful, you'd find out they did. They are eager toward life, there is a certain sparkle in their eye, an erectness to their carriage, and life seems like a pretty interesting adventure to them.
>
> "But by the time they're 65, only one will be rich, four will be financially independent, five will still be working, and 54 will be broke."

These numbers and percentages haven't changed much since they started being tracked. You can look these up yourself. The Social Security Administration has these statistics for 2015 (see Appendix for link):

- Nine out of ten individuals age 65 and older receive Social Security benefits.
- Social Security benefits represent about 39% of the income of the elderly.

That isn't financial independence. That doesn't cover people who are still working so they can maintain their quality of life.

You can find other numbers that say similar things. The widely touted "1% of the population control 95% of the wealth" is another. Like most widely repeated conventional wisdom statistics, this doesn't add up.

The closest I was able to track this down was to a report that translated another report into "The top 1% now owns half the world's wealth" (See Fortune.com link in Appendix.)

Read that more closely, and you'll see it says (paragraph 2): "Worldwide, there are 34 million people who have a U.S. dollar net worth of at least $1 million, or 0.7% of the global adult population, and they account for 45% of global wealth." (Their next sentence fudges it a bit more to arrive at their headline.)

The point is that just becoming a millionaire (which isn't worth as much as it used to be) puts you into an elite class.

One funny observation Earl Nightingale once made was that if you took ten percent of your income every week from the day you started working until 40 years later and never spent it, but saved at a high interest (or reinvested into something with at least a 10% dividend every year) you'd wind up a millionaire by the time you retired.

And then you could live off the interest and arrange to give it all away when you died.

I call it funny only because no one mentions this tidbit in our schooling. If they did, they'd have a society full of millionaires. And if you had a million dollars sitting earning interest for you every month, do you think you'd have to activate your Social Security?

If you track down that actual Credit Suisse report (link in Appendix) you'd find a very interesting fact. The United States still enjoys a very unique role in the world. It is far, far richer than the other countries. Something the media refuses to acknowledge, but Earl Nightingale referred to over and over.

The reason the U.S. is rich is because it's a nation devoted to choice. We have those unique guarantees in our laws, and are the only nation on earth that claims the "pursuit of happiness" in its founding documents.

We are the most prosperous country on Earth mostly because of what we believe. All these Freedoms guaranteed in writing and so on. Ever thought it strange that the countries which incorporate those types of freedom into their governing bodies seem to be more resilient than the rest?

Would you like to look at the difference between North and South Korea again?

Look, I haven't found a bunch of studies that shows where that exact 95%/5% split actually happens.

But dredging up a bunch of studies wouldn't prove much to you at this point. It would actually be a bit contrary to what we've already gone over.

The 95/5 split tends to give you a model that might work to explain a lot of things in this world. It might give you an idea of how valuable a lot of that data you've been carrying around actually is. And how much testing you need to do in order to sort out your life.

Here's the bottom line:

> Did that idea make you feel better?

Try that as a test for now, for all you know and understand to be "true."

The other ways to look at this are:

> 1) Does it make your life simpler? Or

> 2) Does it bring you more peace?

All those questions say the same thing.

THE REVENGE OF THE BUCKET CRABS

Throughout our lives, we are trained to "follow the follower." We are not taught to be entrepreneurs. We are not taught in the fine art of creative thinking. We are not even taught how to make and pursue our own goals.

Rather, our colleges and schools teach us that "you have to go along to get along" and other conformist ideals. We are carefully taught to get a job and let the company plan for your retirement, even if its only a 401-K.

The bulk of American humanity limps along with no real reason to exert the extra effort to "get rich," as there are so many safeguards and "safety nets" in place that it appears it's impossible to outwardly fail at anything during your working years. The surprise is that you are out on your own once you hit retirement. Savings or not, 401K or not. Social Security or not.

Of course in our day and age, the punch lines waiting for you are many: Social Security is mostly or all eaten up by Medicaid payments. If you are laid off close to retirement, most people find it harder to get another job at that age. While the number of businesses being started by the retirement-age crowd is higher than ever, these are being started by "old dogs" who are learning the new skill of entrepreneur on their own dime.

Why has this 90-95% group sat back and waited instead of learning entrepreneurship in their spare time during those earlier 40 years?

The Revenge of the Bucket Crabs

You could call this the revenge of the bucket crabs. The old parable and scientifically-proved fact, is that while a single crab in an open bucket will climb its way out, two or more crabs will keep each other in. And so explains our modern hyper-sensitive, politically-correct culture.

In today's world, all you need is a community organizer to discover any number of wealthy, guilt-ridden patrons and government grants that can support any number of otherwise unemployed minority protesters to popularize your cause in the media. Several people have become well known for their ability to protest in front of major corporations in return for perennial grant funding. Yes, you know who these are.

Why aren't these same people reforming education so that young people of any color or orientation are trained in building businesses, even as a solopreneur? Because they take the easy road out. Short cuts abound in this culture as the majority support the hyper-critical bucket-crab culture.

What Our Economy Is Built On - Crabs

The interesting bottom line is in discovering that the bulk of our consumer-based economy is built on the backs of these same bucket crabs. They buy all the electronic gizmo's, the phones, the clothes, the cars, and get the sub-prime and regular loans for their over-sized houses in neighborhoods they can't afford.

People are trained to live pay-check to pay-check and to pay off college loans and credit card loans right up to the point they can't anymore – which is usually when they are retired willingly or unwillingly.

These are the bucket-crab majority, who make our fast-food restaurant chains and pharmaceutical supply companies rich. These are why there are infomercials and e-mail spam. These are the people who keep watching our advertisement-interrupted television programs as much as 6-8 hours daily.

Why? Because everyone else is doing it. Because their favorite celebrity told them to. Because their politician promised them.

And what do they have to show for it when retired or lose their job? Nothing. They then become fodder for the protest organizers who pay them and feed them if they'll just march here or there. They have to move in with their children. They wind up in a government-paid retirement home.

And they have no one to blame but themselves.

No One to Blame But Ourselves

Look around you. Look at what you read and watch and listen to. How much of this is helpful to you in starting and operating your own business? How much of this helps you create a passive income source to help you live out any lack of a regular job? Most of the social media and magazine articles are either entertainment, hyper-critical, or simply distractive.

Don't look to the evening news for inspirational or motivational material. By actual count of one national news program, they've been arriving in homes for 30 minutes each night, 7 days each week for decades. Out of those 210 minutes, only 5 were dedicated to uplifting material – at 5 minutes before the hour on Friday. (You probably know this network.) That's not even 5% of their programming time. And fully a third of that half-hour time slot was used for what? Advertising, mostly for pharmaceuticals.

And what about their other programming? It's all bucket-crab material. Lots of "reality" type shows. Or you see politicians or celebrities in unusual scenes that would never happen in real life. Or slanted "investigative reporting." All interrupted every 12 minutes or less by yet another pitch.

The Trick to Surviving and Prospering

There's a trick to surviving. It's called *be part of the 5% and profit off the 95%.*

That's not cold or calloused or negative. It's a fact. You can't get people to buy your product unless it's very high quality, very valuable, and very available. Otherwise, you have to constantly bring out new products and spend most of your budget on advertising.

The 95% are trained to go along, get along, and do and buy what they are told. The 5% train themselves to find out what people want and then provide it with better value and distribution than anyone around them. This is how Sam Walton of Wal-Mart became the richest person on earth in his time. This is how Bill Gates, Larry Ellison, Michael Dell, and Warren Buffett make their billions.

It's no secret.

It's a decision they made early on.

You can, too.

It's never too late to quit being an ordinary crab (like most everyone else) and start becoming exceptional.

It's time to get free from that bucket.

THE REASON FOR FAILURE GIVES THE REASON FOR SUCCESS

Nothing new is without risk.

Easy to say, even when you've lived through it.

What they don't tell you is that the worst traps you can run into are in your own mind.

Research found many sources saying the same thing:

- your thoughts become habitual,
- your habits require certain actions,
- your environment is built by your actions to support those habits, and
- your habitual thoughts are then reinforced by the world they create.

Unfortunately, you've been trained since birth to accept conventional wisdom. And this sets your thoughts and mental habits on a very unstable path. (See the quotes in Part 1 about the lies conventional wisdom spreads.)

Only when this accumulated set of beliefs begins routinely failing does a person start to question what they have accepted and then start to rebuild their own world-view.

You can trace most successful people back to a massive failure earlier in life. This is where they had to start thinking on their own, to reconsider all their training, and test it for themselves.

I wrote a very long essay about this in my Living Sensical Manifesto. (Which can be downloaded for free – see Appendix.)

The shorthand is this:

> From birth, you've been trained to not see, to not think, to not act.

Slightly longer explanation:

- You've been trained to accept the world as it is, and how you've been told it works. Your habits are those you copied from people around you as you were growing up and the schools you went to and the jobs you've had.

- These habits were reinforced in your life by what objects and material goods you collected around you. Also, by the entertainment you've watched, heard, and participated in.

- What you've believed in has literally built the world around you. You've become what you thought about. Your world has become what you thought.

The bulk of humanity gets by through incremental improvements. Change is resisted in order to protect everyone from disastrous decisions. This rejection is trained into people as critical thought and comment.

Success is an *exception*.

Exceptional people succeed and create their income because they are decidedly different from almost everyone around them.

They are exceptions to the rule.

Bill Gates, Elon Musk, Thomas Edison, Henry Ford, Warren Buffett, and the top 20 of the richest people on Forbes U.S. list.

All exceptions. Their belief-systems and mental habits are different than people around them, than the people they grew up with. None of these were rich when they started out.

Most didn't finish college and when they did, it was a non-Ivy-League school.

Someone pointed out recently in an interview that "An MBA helps get you a job, it doesn't help you start a business."

Why?

Apparently schools and colleges are busy reinforcing beliefs you are supposed to share and follow.

You can follow this logic by seeing that the winners and top scorers in the National spelling and geography competitions have mostly been home-schooled.

Non-government funded or regulated.

When you start testing your own beliefs and prove them for yourself, taking no one else's word for it, then you become an exception.

Then you have a chance at success.

INTERMISSION

All of this can be heavy going. It's a lot to take in at one time.

If this were a ball game, we'd have a half-time right here. Time for taking a break, hitting the refrigerator, and so on.

Instead of commercials, matching bands, and grinning cheerleaders, we'll instead give you our own offer.

1. A Cheat Sheet

Specifically designed to get you through all this thick training by selecting just the key points to test for yourself.

It's in PDF format and quite easy to understand. Just a few pages, actually.

2. Cutting Room Floor Chapters

This book got too thick, so I thinned it down just to the data you really needed to know. Not that the rest of it wasn't valuable.

But really, you have the rest of your life to soak this in and re-stack your mindset. The best advice for this book is to give it a break for a few days and then start over from the beginning and really test what you study.

To help you distract yourself for those few days, I've got all these chapters set up in PDF format so you can download and study them, put them on your smartphone or tablet, and review them whenever and wherever you want.

3. Special Discounts on Other Versions

I've got a line with the publisher to give you the print versions for 50% off. I'm also looking around to what I can do with the audio versions.

And I want to pass these on to you as well.

4. Upcoming Online Courses

I've also got a full video course in the works which will take all of this and cut it into easier parts to study and understand.

As I've said, this is an introduction to learning how to re-stack your own mindset the way you want it. So it's key for you to be able to really know all the steps you need to take to Make Yourself Great Again.

What's It Going to Cost?

Only your email.

And I won't nag you about things or give you useless offers.

I also don't give anyone else access to my lists. Because you wouldn't want me to treat you that way.

Just go to this link and click on it:

http://livesensical.com/mygajoin/

WHY SCIENTISTS GET IT SO WRONG SO OFTEN

The problem with Scientists may be that they are humans, first.

That means they are subject to the same frailties humans have had before we started our 10,000 years of recorded history.

Here's the two complaints mentioned earlier in this book:

1) 50% of any given scientific study is wrong, that a new scientific discovery is more likely to be disputed and disproved than accepted. (See PLOS link in Appendix.)

2) Science has adopted the materialist mantel almost completely, that is, everything is likened to a machine in all Causes. (See Sheldrake link in Appendix.)

Any scientists doing research has to conform in order to get funding and advance their career. They have to get the approval of their peers in order to continue research in their given fields.

Government-employed scientists (those what work at publicly-funded universities) have to "publish or perish" in order to get raises or keep working there. They have to submit papers to peer-reviewed journals annually.

Look back on Kuhn's "paradigm shift" concept (link in Appendix) and you'll see in the discussion that there is a huge social factor present with the move from one model to the newer one.

In short, our very human scientists are too often following followers rather than leading research into new and novel areas where questions remain unanswered. Far from being new, this is the continuing approach for Science since the subject was invented.

It's normal for people to view new data in light of the models they've already adopted.

Like politicians need voter-approval to continue their careers, scientists need their peers to approve their work in order to continue theirs.

So the breakthroughs are rare, exceptions. Much as we've already discussed.

Successes in scientific research come rarely, because those scientists have to think things differently and be relatively immune from social pressures to conform. They must escape the influence of their fellow Bucket Crabs.

Business is faster than science to change, because of two factors: a) they are capable of greater change than laws can be passed to stop them, and b) they frame their new products and services in the age-old desires humankind has been running on since before we developed writing.

I've seen businesses change their product, rebuild their assembly lines, and revamp their marketing during the time a bill was just being considered in committee. And in other cases, simply changing the packaging itself would allow them to escape the law. This is all in addition to their lobbyists enabling loopholes in those bills through timely donations to those same politicians, as well as dragging those bills through the courts when other efforts fail.

Marketing (particularly Eugene Schwartz) has said to align your product or service to the base desires your public has. You frame the argument in terms of their needs and wants, namely what they need emotionally, and the wanted features of the product which makes it rationally a "good buy." Again, people decides emotionally and justify rationally. Just the way we are.

Scientists are no different. The emotional needs they have for acceptance will require them to rationalize their arguments to conform to the scientific community their studies put them in.

(This explains how "Global Warming" has become "Climate Change" and why this new paradigm isn't widely accepted outside of government agencies and broadcast media.)

The materialism approach puts blinders on any sort of study which isn't mechanically cause-and-effect driven. We'll see shortly that the oldest-surviving philosophies on this planet actually have three additional ways to study any phenomenon.

Science is then much like running a four-cylinder car with a single piston.

For now, just know that you need to test everything given to you as "resolved fact" and "beyond debate."

Authorities need to be questioned before you follow them, blindly or with eyes wide open.

THOUGHTS ARE CONTAGIOUS, AND SO ARE EMOTIONAL HABITS.

You can pick up other people's bad habits by just being around them.

Weird, but true. No, you won't find this in most books.

This is because the beliefs you hold are shared, whether you like it or not.

I first ran into this from one of these "accidental millionaire" Internet Marketers. He had built his income from a business built on short-cuts that took advantage of people's fears to "make money." He said thoughts are contagious. And I didn't believe him. But when I got into some classic self-help books, I found that same datum resurfacing.

Napoleon Hill covered this in his Think and Grow Rich 1945 sequel, "The Master Keys to Success." There he produced a concept he called "Cosmic Habitforce." This idea simply is that both good and bad habits are available for anyone to pick up from the people around them.

To fully grasp this, you need to review Chapter 13, "The Brain", from his *Think and Grow Rich*. There he explores a concept that the brain is more a transmitting and receiving station for all thought.

Other studies, such as those by independent researcher Jose Silva in the '70's found that when the brain is producing delta wavelengths (just above sleep) that telepathic and other pre-cognitive abilities can be demonstrated.

Hill emphasizes the need to carefully select those who you associate and work with, as any critical habit of theirs will "rub off on you."

Just as similarly, a person who practices a positive mental attitude can lift the spirits in an office or workplace. As well, a gloomy and depressed person will make all those around him feel worse to some degree. Claude M. Bristol warns about this several times in his book.

Habits are just routinely continued actions over time. Mental habits are formed by using the same emotional responses to any given situation, over and over. These develop a patterned response to any given situation. Emotions are programmed this way. Your programming is developed by watching your parents, teachers, friends, and family. You keep seeing them use the same reaction over and over. You then adopt their emotional responses as your own.

Worst yet, if you have just encountered a high-stress situation, it may only take a single response that is adopted as the pattern. Particularly where you're belief-system has failed to prepare you for that situation.

In there somewhere is the explanation for PTSD, both military and civilian.

Emotions and feelings are different, but they are often confused. Both are under the control of the person. The word emotion itself means "motion out." This is a response to outside action. Emotions are generated. Most people have conditioned responses that they use to generate the "appropriate" emotional response to any given situation.

Feelings are more perceptions. They are internal and usually not voiced or communicated. You may feel sad, but your emotional response may be "grief." You can feel happy, but an emotional response would be laughing, smiling, or exhilaration.

Where something is a state, it's usually a feeling. Where you are in action, this is usually an emotion – again, literally "motion out."

A lot of our feelings are classified using terms that are actually emotions.

But this doesn't mean you are an automaton. It only says that you may have swallowed some programmed responses and adopted them as habits to get through life. Your emotions are forms of communication with others.

Psychologist William James gave us a trick to sort these out, and to take more control over our own lives, emotions, and feelings:

"We need only in cold blood *act* as if the thing in question were real, and it will become infallibly real by growing into such a connection with our life that it will become real. It will become so knit with habit and emotion that our interests in it will be those which characterize belief."

In short, act happy and you'll start feeling happy. Start smiling and you'll find some reason to smile.

Releasing is another way to achieve a calm, cheerful state of being.

You don't have to get habitually angry when something upsets you.

But do watch for the patterns others give you in their own responses. Like a sneeze spreads germs, a tirade can spread an angry habit across the whole office.

If you want to inoculate an office, set a good example of facing problems with a cheerful expression and honesty.

W. Clement Stone was known to react to anything that happened with, "That's Good!" and then go about finding what was good about that situation, whether it was positive or negative at the outset. Shortly, he would indeed find what was good in that scene.

He was a great believer in keeping a positive mental attitude at all times, even writing several books in this area on his own and with Napoleon Hill as a co-author. Stone lived to be 100. Every morning he would look at himself in a mirror and state, "I feel healthy, I feel happy, I feel terrific!" and start the day with a smile and cheerfulness.

You can try this yourself, right now. See if you can't change the way you've been feeling.

CRITICISM IS PROBABLY MORE CONTAGIOUS THAN HAPPINESS

Feeling bad has its own rewards.

That probably is why it is so common in our society.

Simply: Bucket Crabs need help to be effective. Misery loves company.

The truly weird thing is that people who develop a constant critical outlook never are really happy. They can never find peace as long as they keep going that way.

And so, they develop substitutes of getting a lot of "stuff" into their lives. Lots of cars and clothes and time-share condo's to take expensive vacations in.

But the old stories hold true. You cannot serve both God and Stuff. Money can't buy love.

And you'll search to find all these people who have attained high states of awareness (Zen, Peak Experience) who actually made it a point to get rid of all sorts of stuff right out of their lives. There's a new trend of minimalism and "de-cluttering" that address this again in our modern days.

Yet (if we accept what's been covered so far) we're vastly outnumbered by Bucket Crabs than we are by exceptional and successful people.

And those thoughts and mental habits are being broadcast at us continually. 95 out of 100 people we meet wants us to fail. We're receiving these ideas all the time as well as through the media we watch, unless we are highly discerning and disciplined with our inputs.

Is all this work to be successful worth it?

After all, there are far more examples of government-sponsored assistance and the ever-present cushion that keeps anyone from really failing (even if it also means they won't have anything above a subsistence level of existence.)

Is that our future then - to simply live out our lives in some sort of Welfare state, sharing particularly witty and critical remarks from our old-age home rockers or easy chairs? And our amusement will be simply watching whatever is on TV without the ability or reason to even get up and change the channel?

Our problem is that we still really don't know how or why this is happening. We still don't really know how to handle these scenes that are tearing us down perhaps harder than we can build ourselves up.

In our failures, this is particularly true. So are the real successes simply "accidental millionaires" who "build their business" on psycho-babble?

Was the misquoted "Nice Guys Finish Last" far more accurate than the original?

I would remind you of Earl Nightingale's "Strangest Secret":

"We Become What We Think About."

It's still your choice what to think and who you "hang" with...

DO YOU GET SUPERCHARGED OR A SUPER VILLAIN?

One of those hot, humid days Missouri has in summer gave me yet another clue. It was on my own bookshelf and I'd never read it.

Apparently, I'd bought it at some point before, but never opened it. I didn't recall.

Have you ever been touched by coincidental thought? That odd, intuitional idea that crosses your mind and you can follow or not. If you follow, you can have answers. One of the books for this course, "Magic of Believing" says to go ahead follow and why.

In this case, after I had changed the title of this book to have the word "Belief" in it, I saw this book "How We Believe"by Michael Shermer and the idea took me that this could be something useful here, so I picked it up. Much of the book on leafing through it was filled with talks of God and Science, and had multi-syllabic pronunicamentos that rendered it hard to follow. I'd never heard of the author

I flipped to the Table of Contents and saw a chapter that looked interested. Reading just a few pages, it hit me: we are each pots filled to overflowing with belief. To change your belief, you apparently have to substitute out some other belief. (Like a full stew pot that needs carrots added will mean taking out some of the potatoes.) How much belief we can hold isn't known. But we believe regardless.

This is the old practice of needing from 28 to 40 days in order to change a habit - by doing a new action every time you experience a certain situation.

The trick is that we constantly want to believe. It's built into our human system, much like we know to take a breath when we are born and keep doing it until the day we die. Much like we start circulating blood when still part of our Mother, yet can continue doing this after our other organs have failed.

In sheer metaphysical terms, our beliefs start before our birth and continue after death. How strong these are, or how much they are tied to the physical body, we cannot say.

There are stories of beliefs which transcend time. José Silva's work in active meditation and brainwave activity found a person can move into communication with others that apparently occurs outside of real time. Events can be known and predicted which haven't happened. All sorts of interesting "extra-sensory perception" can occur. More importantly, they can be explained and duplicated, repeated at will.

The question again is not who is doing this, but why anyone would want to.

The hidden plot here is that anyone could actually supercharge their own abilities if they were to simply study their own beliefs and change those which were limiting. Ultimately, any number of abilities could surface.

Both Silva and Bristol had strong warnings about using these abilities only for good.

But apparently they didn't need to warn us as much as they did. I've told you earlier that the people who act destructive are also self-destructive. The longest-living people are generally peaceful and easy-going. While irritable people have been known to die of a bad temper, due to physical manifestations of stroke, heart attack, or brain aneurysm.

To the degree someone is going down the line of negative/destructive belief, that person is killing themselves off.

W. Clement Stone may have proved the concept of a positive mental attitude increasing longevity with that affirmation to his reflection in the mirror every day.

In that line of thought, we come back again to the point of simply filling our lives with good feelings, such as peace. Developing a habit of purposely "feeling good." Too many of the most respected philosophers through history have told us to do just that.

The stories of Jesus being taught in foreign lands before he returned for those last few years in and around Jerusalem might make the case of someone transforming his own beliefs into a super-charged state.

Certainly Max Freedom Long found that the Polynesians who followed their ancient beliefs were able to do what we now call miracles. And our beliefs in technology have enabled us to do what would have been called miracles in an earlier age. Our smart phones, as primitive as they are, now allow us to do the Star Trek communicator thing, or the Dick Tracy wrist watch thing.

But "thoughts are things" as Prentice Mulford wrote.

Not to put too light a touch on it, certainly the beliefs of Hitler, Mussolini, and Stalin caused tons of suffering and death for multitudes. The warped beliefs of those following ISIS and Al-Quaeda are working to drive that area back into desert, as well as killing innocent bystanders as they try to force the Apocalypse to appear now. (And the beliefs of our own broadcast news agencies are assisting them, as well as certain of our politicians.)

Consider also that bullies turn into cowards when faced. For all the mass killings by deranged individuals, there are stories where someone else faced them down, saving lives. Controversial as it may seem, when a bully with a gun is confronted by someone else with a gun, then the bully quits.

Both sides of this mental coin have beliefs. It's your beliefs which can make you suicidally destructive. It's your beliefs which can take you to heights of supernatural ability and unstoppable internal peace, for you and those around you.

Beliefs are like choices. They are as natural as breathing, and you can't stop doing any of them. How you breathe can be modified, what you choose and how you believe can be changed.

You can supercharge yourself, or become a super-villain, or remain super-mundane. That's choice.

POSTSCRIPT

Now that you've seen what passes for the "real' world, it's time to look behind the curtain to find the actual world and who's been running it.

Surprises await...

PREVIEW OF PART 3

Finally the villains in this new world you've been studying are revealed.

But getting your wits around understanding them is again a "riddle wrapped in a mystery, inside an enigma."

We are again going to be finding solutions hidden in plain sight, actually published in popular works every decade since books began being printed (and actually when they were still being hand-copied.)

Again, we are seeing that as we've been taught to not look, to not think, and to not act is exactly what these villains have been wanting us to do.

The few who have escaped that mold are the true heroes. These few are both hated and feared by their enemies because they do not follow the paths that everyone else do.

They seek to "follow the different drummer that they hear, however measured or far away."

These heroes cannot be controlled. They are the few who employ the many.

And we are also going to see some of tragic heroes who have lived in our own times. What they thought is what they became. And those thoughts seemed to literally create the world around them. They didn't worry about living the world as others taught them. They instead followed that different drummer's music.

Not all exceptional people are successes according to the standards of the world.

Yet you and I and everyone can be a hero(ine) if we choose to do so. That path is difficult, and you won't find a lot of people to help you make your journey. The villains have many unwitting accomplices that surround you and slow you down at every step.

Yet people do it every generation. Many only start after they are in their 40's. But succeed they do.

We'll also see the interesting story of how goals have been proved to be a very lucrative investment, if you'll only write them down.

There are miracles to be had.

Beliefs are powerful things. What are yours?

APPENDIX

LINKS FOR PART 1 & 2

How Science gets it half wrong every time:

- PLOS article:
  http://journals.plos.org/plosmedicine/article?id=10.1371/journal.pmed.0020124

- Readable version in The Guardian
  https://www.theguardian.com/science/occams-corner/2013/sep/17/scientific-studies-wrong

- or The Economist
  http://www.economist.com/news/leaders/21588069-scientific-research-has-changed-world-now-it-needs-change-itself-how-science-goes-wrong

How Science fudges its processes – Rupert Sheldrake:

- Rupert Sheldrake on wikipedia -
  https://en.wikipedia.org/wiki/Rupert_Sheldrake

- His banned TED talk -
  https://steemit.com/science/@morpheustitania/the-science-delusion-banned-ted-talk - fortunately that page also has a partial transcript.

Surveys of government trust by their people:

- http://www.people-press.org/2015/11/23/1-trust-in-government-1958-2015/

- http://www.gallup.com/poll/5392/trust-government.aspx

Reports that media isn't trusted:

- http://bigstory.ap.org/article/35c595900e0a4ffd99f bdc48a336a6d8/poll-vast-majority-americans-dont-trust-news-media and

- Gallup http://www.gallup.com/poll/185927/americans-trust-media-remains-historical-low.aspx

Get Your Self Scam Free

http://livesensical.com/scamfree

Lester Levenson and Releasing Technique

http://sedona.org

http://releasetechnique.com

http://www.lesterandme.com/

A collection of various links about Levenson and releasing can be found at: http://dumpem.com

Social Security Statistics 2015

https://www.ssa.gov/news/press/basicfact.html

"Top 1% Own 50% of World's Wealth"

http://fortune.com/2015/10/14/1-percent-global-wealth-credit-suisse/

https://publications.credit-uisse.com/tasks/render/file/?fileID=F2425415-DCA7-80B8-EAD989AF9341D47E

Thomas Kuhn's Paradigm Shift

https://en.wikipedia.org/wiki/Paradigm_shift

About Opal Whitely

- *The Fantastic Tale of Opal Whiteley* by Steve McQuiddy
http://www.intangible.org/Acrobat/FeaturesPDF/Opal.pdf

- KBOO radio program:
http://www.kboo.fm/media/31559-opal-whiteley

Study of Goal Achievement by Dominican University

http://www.dominican.edu/academics/ahss/undergraduate-programs/psych/faculty/assets-gail-matthews/researchsummary2.pdf

Dell Theory of Conflict Prevention (Thomas Friedman)

https://en.wikipedia.org/wiki/The_World_Is_Flat#Dell_theory_of_Conflict_Prevention

BIBLIOGRAPHY

Brande, Dorothea
>   *Wake Up and Live!*
>   *Becoming a Writer*

Bristol, Claude M.
>   *The Magic of Believing*

Byrne, Rhonda
>   *The Secret (DVD)*

Campbell, Joseph
>   *Hero With a Thousand Faces*

Carson, Rachel
>   *Silent Spring*

Cialdini, Robert
>   *Influence*

Coyne, Shawn
>   *Story Grid*

Ehrlich, Paul
>   *Population Bomb*

Gladwell, Malcolm
>   *Outliers*
>   *Blink*

Hill, Napoleon
>   *Think and Grow Rich*
>   *Master Key to Riches*

10 Lessons in Cosmic Habitforce

James, William

The Principles of Psychology

The Will to Believe

Jones, James Breckenridge

If You Can Count to Four

King, Dr. Serge Kahili

The Seven Principles of Huna (lecture)

King, Stephen

On Writing

Long, Max Freedom

Introduction to Huna

Huna: Recovering the Ancient Magic

Maslow, Abraham

A Theory of Human Motivation

Nightingale, Earl

The Strangest Secret (transcript)

How to Completely Change Your Life in 30 Seconds

Ponder, Catherine

The Dynamic Laws of Prosperity

Schwartz, Eugene

Breakthrough Advertising

Breakthrough Copywriter (based on his talks)

Vogler, Chris

The Writer's Journey

Whitely, Opal

    The Journal of an Understanding Heart

Worstell, Robert C

    Go Thunk Yourself

    Go Thunk Yourself, Again

    What Jesus Really Said

*The **Living Sensical Manifesto** may be downloaded at no cost (or even opt-in) at: https://calm.li/LSmanifesto*

ACKNOWLEDGMENTS

Many thanks to Ed Grunzel, Simone Agarrat, RT, Sarah M, and Vasant Alfred for helping me get this book ready. You are appreciated more than you know.

INDEX

BONUS 2

I'd like to give you a few more things to help you out:

00) *All of the bonuses for Part 1*, including that book itself and its audiobook.

0) *A Cheat Sheet for Part 2*, where you get a list of the key datums covered, all in a simple PDF. This is so you can test the data you've read for yourself.

1) *Access to a member's only library* of references which give the background and more tools to enable you improve your own success chances.

2) *An upcoming course* that can assist you in changing your mental habits and get failure -free if you want. (No charge to subscribers.)

3) *A personal line to the author f*or any assistance you want in learning to apply this book.

4) *...And advanced offers plus discounts* for the rest of the books in this series, as well as other versions such as audio and even video versions.

All you have to do is to sign up using the link below.

Do this now. Click or type this into your browser for instant access:

http://livesensical.com/mygajoin/

www.ingramcontent.com/pod-product-compliance
Lightning Source LLC
Chambersburg PA
CBHW021929170526
45157CB00005B/2242